WEEKLY **WR** READER®
EARLY LEARNING LIBRARY

Things with Wings

THE LIFE CYCLE OF A
HUMMINGBIRD

by JoAnn Early Macken

Reading consultant: Susan Nations, M.Ed.,
author/literacy coach/consultant in literacy development

Please visit our web site at: **www.earlyliteracy.cc**
For a free color catalog describing Weekly Reader® Early Learning Library's
list of high-quality books, call 1-877-445-5824 (USA) or 1-800-387-3178 (Canada).
Weekly Reader® Early Learning Library's fax: (414) 336-0164.

Library of Congress Cataloging-in-Publication Data

Macken, JoAnn Early, 1953-
    The life cycle of a hummingbird / by JoAnn Early Macken.
        p. cm. — (Things with wings)
    Includes index.
    ISBN 0-8368-6383-6 (lib. bdg.)
    ISBN 0-8368-6390-9 (softcover)
    1. Hummingbirds—Life cycles—Juvenile literature. I. Title.
QL696.A558M33   2006
598.7′64—dc22   2005026610

This edition first published in 2006 by
Weekly Reader® Early Learning Library
A Member of the WRC Media Family of Companies
330 West Olive Street, Suite 100
Milwaukee, WI 53212 USA

Copyright © 2006 by Weekly Reader® Early Learning Library

Managing editor: Dorothy L. Gibbs
Art direction: Tammy West
Photo research: Diane Laska-Swanke

Photo credits: Cover, © Ray Coleman/Visuals Unlimited; p. 5 © Robert & Jean Pollock/
Visuals Unlimited; p. 7 © Tom and Pat Leeson; pp. 9, 17, 19 © Richard Day/Daybreak
Imagery; pp. 11, 21 © Charles Melton/Visuals Unlimited; p. 13 © Tom Vezo/naturepl.com;
p. 15 © Steve Maslowski/Visuals Unlimited

Printed in the United States of America

1 2 3 4 5 6 7 8 9 10 09 08 07 06

Note to Educators and Parents

Reading is such an exciting adventure for young children! They are beginning to integrate their oral language skills with written language. To encourage children along the path to early literacy, books must be colorful, engaging, and interesting; they should invite the young reader to explore both the print and the pictures.

Things with Wings is a new series designed to help children read about fascinating animals, all of which have wings. In each book, young readers will learn about the life cycle of the featured animal, as well as other interesting facts.

Each book is specially designed to support the young reader in the reading process. The familiar topics are appealing to young children and invite them to read — and re-read — again and again. The full-color photographs and enhanced text further support the student during the reading process.

In addition to serving as wonderful picture books in schools, libraries, homes, and other places where children learn to love reading, these books are specifically intended to be read within an instructional guided reading group. This small group setting allows beginning readers to work with a fluent adult model as they make meaning from the text. After children develop fluency with the text and content, the book can be read independently. Children and adults alike will find these books supportive, engaging, and fun!

— Susan Nations, M.Ed., author, literacy coach, and consultant in literacy development

Hummingbirds are the smallest birds. A hummingbird is as small as a bar of soap. Its nest is tiny, too. Some nests are as small as walnut shells.

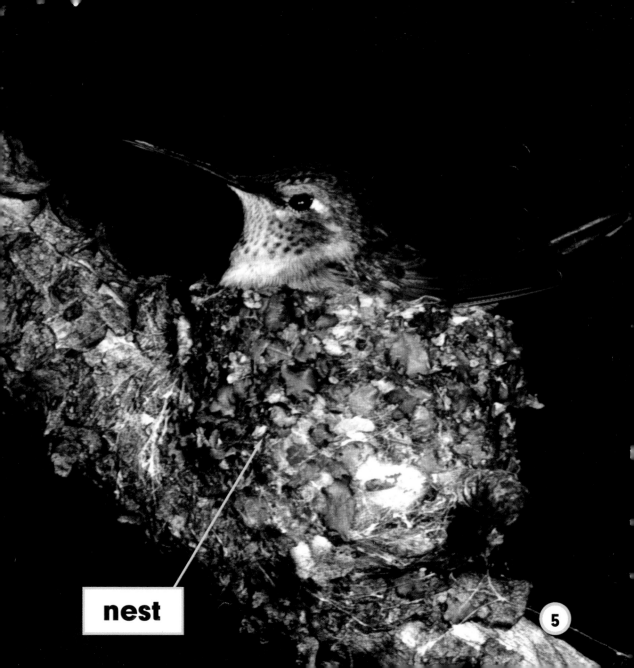

nest

5

Baby hummingbirds hatch from eggs. Their mother feeds them many times a day. She feeds them for three or four weeks. Then they must find their own food.

7

A baby hummingbird has thin, dark feathers. In three or four weeks, it can fly. It is ready to leave the nest.

9

All hummingbirds have long, thin beaks. Some are straight. Some curve. A hummingbird pokes its beak into a flower to feed. It sticks out its tongue to drink nectar.

beak

Hummingbirds often keep flying while they eat. They **hover**, or fly in one place, to drink nectar. Hummingbirds also eat insects.

Most hummingbirds do not walk. To move even a short way, they fly. Their flapping wings hum as they fly. Some people call them "hummers."

Most male hummingbirds have bright spots of shiny feathers. One kind has shiny green feathers with a bright red spot on its neck.

17

A male hummingbird's bright colors help it find a mate. Male hummingbirds also sing to find mates.

A female hummingbird lays two white eggs. The eggs are as small as peas or beans. The eggs will hatch in about two weeks. Most hummingbirds can live about ten years.

The Life Cycle of a Hummingbird

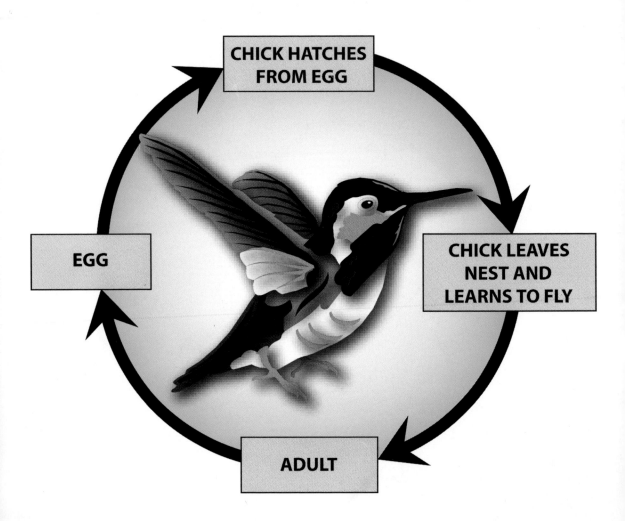

CHICK HATCHES FROM EGG

EGG

CHICK LEAVES NEST AND LEARNS TO FLY

ADULT

Glossary

hatch — to break out of an egg

hover — to fly in one place

mate — partner

migrate — to move to a new place from time to time

nectar — a sweet liquid in flowers

Index

About the Author

JoAnn Early Macken is the author of two rhyming picture books, *Sing-Along Song* and *Cats on Judy*, and more than eighty nonfiction books for children. Her poems have appeared in several children's magazines. A graduate of the M.F.A. in Writing for Children and Young Adults Program at Vermont College, she lives in Wisconsin with her husband and their two sons.